RAND

Germany's Contribution to Peacekeeping

Issues and Outlook

Ronald D. Asmus

Prepared for the
Office of the Secretary of Defense

National Defense
Research Institute

WITHDRAWN

This report examines the German debate over peacekeeping, how Germany is moving to shed the political and military constraints on the use of the German armed forces, and the potential role that Germany might play in future peace support operations. How Germany has sought to come to terms with the challenge of peace-keeping operations in the post–Cold War era is an important story in its own right. However, given Germany's influential role in Europe and beyond, the German experience sets an important precedent and may offer some insights for other countries that face primarily political constraints to increasing their contribution to peacekeeping operations.

This report was written for the project "Increasing the Availability and Effectiveness of Non-U.S. Forces for Multinational Peace Operations," conducted within the International Security and Defense Policy Center of RAND's National Defense Research Institute (NDRI), a federally funded research and development center sponsored by the Office of the Secretary of Defense, the Joint Staff, and the defense agencies. The project is sponsored by the Office of the Deputy Assistant Secretary of Defense for Peacekeeping and Peace Enforcement Policy.

CONTENTS

SUMMARY

In July 1994, the German Supreme Court ruled that there was no constitutional ban on the use of the German armed forces beyond Germany's borders. On the same day of the German Supreme Court ruling, the German Defense Minister also issued planning guidance for the future development of the Bundeswehr. In March 1995, the German cabinet approved a final detailed plan for the restructuring of the Bundeswehr, including the individual services, for a new and broader spectrum of missions. Taken together, they present a de facto blueprint of German plans to build military capabilities from which a future German contribution to peacekeeping will be drawn.

Since the end of the Cold War, Germany has moved further and faster in shedding the constraints on the use of the German armed forces than many observers had initially anticipated. To be sure, the debate over the future restructuring and use of the German armed forces is not over. However, the legal question mark over the use of German armed forces beyond territorial defense has been lifted and many of the political constraints have dissipated. The terms of the debate have clearly shifted under the pressure of real world events and in the face of a new set of political dynamics. A new political and strategic rationale for the Bundeswehr has officially been embraced, one that explicitly includes the full spectrum of both peace support and possible combat missions.

The Bundeswehr has embarked on a reorientation and restructuring process that has been rightly termed the second birth of the Bundeswehr. When fully implemented, it is designed to give it a modest but potent capability to project military forces and operate as a key ally in future coalition operations beyond Germany's borders. To be sure, it remains to be seen how well plans for the new Bundeswehr hold up both in German politics and in the real world, for a number of key issues have yet to be resolved in practice. Nevertheless, German participation in future peace support operations, as well as combat operations beyond Germany's borders, is no longer a question of whether but when, where, and how.

Several aspects of the Bundeswehr's restructuring are especially relevant for Bonn's possible future involvement in peacekeeping missions. The German Bundeswehr will now be reduced from 370,000 to 340,000 by 1996. This will include 290,000 Main Defense Forces (MDF) and 50,000 Crisis Reaction Forces (CRF). Although senior German military leaders emphasize that Germany's MDF continue to constitute the backbone of Germany's contribution to NATO and the balance of power in the heart of Europe, the creation of these new Crisis Reaction Forces is the main new development and the Bundeswehr's top strategic and modernization priority. It is from these new capabilities that the German peacekeeping capabilities will flow.

The CRF have three missions. They are designed, first, to contribute to territorial defense. Second, they are also available for in-region defense throughout the territory of the Atlantic Alliance, as well as to contribute to the future crisis management capabilities of the North Atlantic Treaty Organization (NATO) or the Western European Union (WEU). Third and finally, it is from these assets that the future German peacekeeping contribution under either the United Nations (UN) or the Organization for Security and Cooperation in Europe (OSCE) will be drawn. In the words of the Inspector General of the Bundeswehr, General Klaus Naumann, the purpose of the CRF is to enable Germany to participate in peacekeeping and crisis management operations that allow Bonn to keep conflict away from its territory.

These CRF will include:

- Six mechanized, light, and air-mobile brigades with their combat support and logistics components, as well as the German component of the Franco-German brigade.

- Six air force squadrons for attack, air defense, and reconnaissance missions, two mixed surface-to-air missile (SAM) wings, and three mixed air transport wings as well as helicopters for search and rescue missions.

- Two naval task forces of two to three frigates each with the corresponding mine warfare and naval air arm assets. The German navy will also have the capability to transport a small peacekeeping contingent—about one army battalion—and to serve as command headquarters for that unit.

The CRF are designed to simultaneously allow for one major operation (i.e., up to an army division along with corresponding air assets) and simultaneous participation in smaller missions—e.g., peacekeeping, humanitarian assistance, and evacuations. These forces will be designed to meet NATO readiness standards—i.e., small numbers will be ready to deploy within 48 hours, others in 3–7 days, and the entire contingent within 15–30 days.

Because of these higher standards (and because of the political sensitivities associated with a conscript army engaged in missions beyond territorial defense), 80–85 percent will consist of professional soldiers. The remaining conscripts will consist of volunteers. The maximal duration of a mission is foreseen as six months. How long will it take for the Bundeswehr to implement these plans? German Ministry of Defense (MoD) officials state that two battalions will be ready for peacekeeping by the end of 1994 with one full brigade available in 1995. All CRF are scheduled to be operational by 1998/1999.

Training is also central to how the Bundeswehr prepares itself for future peacekeeping missions. New policy guidance has been issued for the training of German army units for future peace support operations. Although the guidance emphasized that training for peace support missions should be seen as a complement to standard training, not as a substitute, it remains to be seen whether the intense but short training periods currently envisioned are sufficient to prepare units for future missions.

In addition to earmarking units for certain types of missions, the Bundeswehr has established a special school in Hammelburg for UN peace support operations. In addition to familiarizing officers and noncommissioned officers (NCOs) with UN peace support procedures, this school will provide specialized training in a variety of areas—staff officers for UN missions, military observers, logistics specialists, military policemen, and combat engineers. It will offer special intensive courses (usually three weeks in duration) for units preparing to deploy in peace support missions. The courses will be taught in English and will include non-German participants. German officers will also be trained at the UN Logistic Officer Course (UNLOC) in Norway as well as the UN Military Police Course (UNMILPOC) in Denmark.

Finally, the Bundeswehr is reorganizing its command structures to enable it to operate better outside of NATO. Senior MoD officials have singled out this issue, along with logistics and training, as one of the key areas that the Bundeswehr must make its top priorities. In January 1995, Bonn created a joint service command and control center for future peacekeeping missions. Established provisionally for a one-year period, it has been added as a new staff division to the existing armed forces command structure. Its responsibilities will include operational planning as well as the operational command of future peacekeeping missions. Its future status will be reviewed after an initial one-year trial period.

German officials and parliamentarians have openly debated the criteria that should be used for deciding when to say yes or no to a request for German forces for a peacekeeping operation. The principles thus far articulated in public and private by leading officials in both the foreign and defense ministries include:

1. Germany has no automatic obligation to the UN or OSCE. Bonn retains the right to refuse requests and to decide its involvement case by case.

2. Germany's future military role will be determined by values and German national interests as well as its alliance obligations.

3. Germany's priority will be peacekeeping missions in and around Europe. Multilateral involvement, especially of Bonn's allies in NATO and the WEU, will be critical. The greater the participation of Bonn's allies, the more likely German participation will be.

4. History should not determine where German troops can go—i.e., German troops can go where the Wehrmacht has been, *provided* that their presence is viewed as a stabilizing factor. The consent of the parties involved in the conflict will be an important factor.

5. The principle of subsidiarity—i.e., regional organizations and powers—should be in the forefront of resolving regional crises.

6. There must be a credible political prospect for the success of the mission. The greater the dangers the more crucial it is that there be a clear timetable and concept for political success.

7. There must be a requirement for a political mandate through the OSCE or the UN as well as an achievable set of operational goals. Following the Somalian experience, German officials emphasized that it may be better not to get involved in an operation than to have to withdraw in failure.

Several key questions remain unanswered. The first, and in many ways most important, question is how will Germans define their interests and where will they see them as sufficiently engaged to justify German participation in future peacekeeping missions.?

A second crucial and as yet unanswered question is how well the Bundeswehr will perform in future peace support operations. Bonn has now resolved the political and legal issues that had heretofore constrained Germany from assuming such a role. The German Ministry of Defense has designed a blueprint to create significant new capabilities from which Bonn could contribute to future peacekeeping missions. Yet, these same forces are in theory supposed to be able to handle the full range of crisis response and peacekeeping missions beyond territorial defense. There are important qualitative differences that, in turn, pose very different demands in terms of preparing German forces for the future.

Third, Germany is starting to experience the kinds of debates that will sound all too familiar to an American audience. How does one decide criteria for future missions in practice? How involved should civilians become in detailed military operational planning? What is the proper balance between executive and legislative authority in decisionmaking processes? No doubt the German debate will also soon experience controversies over the relative merits of limited vs.

decisive force. Germans will approach all these issues through their own optic, one that is shaped by their own history and experience. Germany is at the beginning of a new learning curve, forced to deal with an entire set of issues it was spared from facing in the past due to the limits mandated on the Bundeswehr.

Fourth, the evolution of German public opinion on this issue will be crucial. A series of public opinion polls commissioned by RAND since the fall of the Berlin Wall have shown that Germans are defining a new set of national interests beyond their border. By overwhelming margins they support the principle of German participation in peacekeeping operations. However, the German public remains skittish about the use of the Bundeswehr in combat missions. Support on this front remains low, although it has started to inch up. Political leadership will be essential to insure that this shift continues.

Germany has come a long way since the collapse of communism in redefining its foreign policy interests and role and determining how a new Bundeswehr fits into that broader vision. The crux of the practical political problem for Bonn is that when it does decide to employ the Bundeswehr in peace support operations, the rationale and German interest must be clear, its key allies must be involved under a clear mandate, and such missions must be a success lest the emerging new consensus in favor of a German military role be shattered.

ACKNOWLEDGMENTS

The author would like to thank the German Ministry of Defense for its help in collecting a variety of research materials used in this report. The author would also like to thank Jed Peters for a very helpful review of an earlier version of this report.

Chapter One

INTRODUCTION

This report examines the German debate over peacekeeping. How Germany has sought to come to terms with the challenge of peacekeeping operations in the post–Cold War era is an important story in its own right. While many aspects of the German experience are undoubtedly sui generis, given the country's influential role in Europe and beyond, the German experience sets an important precedent and may offer insights for other countries that face primarily political constraints to increasing their contribution to peacekeeping operations.

Since the end of the Cold War, Germany has moved further and faster in shedding the constraints on the use of the German armed forces than many observers initially expected. To be sure, the debate over the future restructuring and use of the German armed forces is not over. However, the legal question mark over the use of German armed forces beyond territorial defense has been lifted and many of the political constraints have been diluted if not removed. For example, whereas a few years ago many German politicians talked about limiting the future role of the Bundeswehr to traditional consensual peacekeeping missions and also excluded the possibility of the Bundeswehr ever being deployed to areas where the German Wehrmacht had been during the Second World War, now the debate encompasses the full range of possible missions for the Bundeswehr and the German government has officially stated that history will not determine where the Bundeswehr can or cannot be deployed.

The terms of the debate have clearly shifted under the pressure of real world events and in the face of a new set of political dynamics. A

1

new political and strategic rationale for the Bundeswehr has officially been embraced, one that explicitly includes the full spectrum of both peace support and possible combat missions. The Bundeswehr has embarked on a reorientation and restructuring process that has been rightly termed the second birth of the Bundeswehr. When fully implemented, it is designed to give the Bundeswehr a modest but potent capability to project military forces and operate as a key ally in future coalition operations beyond Germany's borders. To be sure, the blueprint for a new Bundeswehr is still being implemented, and it remains to be seen how well it holds up both in German politics and in the real world, for a number of key issues have yet to be resolved in practice. Nevertheless, German participation in future peace support operations, as well as combat operations beyond Germany's borders, is no longer a question of whether but of when, where, and how.

Germany's potential peacekeeping contribution must be seen in conjunction with the overall debate over redefining German security policy and defense policy for the post–Cold War era. Germany's unification, the collapse of communism, and the unraveling of the USSR radically changed Europe's geopolitical landscape and Germany's role in it. The Federal Republic was transformed from a divided front-line state located at the East-West divide into the largest and in many ways most powerful country located in the heart of Europe. One of the traditional consumers of security during the Cold War, Germany now faces the challenge of becoming a producer of security in the post–Cold War era.

The implications of this dramatic transformation are at the heart of the new debate over future German foreign and defense policy. If the old German Question has been answered with German unification, then the new German Question is what role should a reunited Germany now assume in Europe and beyond? How should a reunited Germany define its interests in Europe's new landscape? What institutions and instruments will Germans turn to as they pursue those interests? How will German attitudes toward the use of power and military force evolve in the years ahead? How should the Bundeswehr be redesigned to meet these challenges? What should be the proper balance between executive and legislative authority as Germany establishes the proper modalities for future decisionmaking? How strong is public support for this new German military role?

Peacekeeping has been at the center of this new debate. In the immediate wake of the collapse of communism, it emerged as the key venue through which Germans started to define a new strategic and military role beyond territorial defense. In part this reflected the initial surge of support and enthusiasm for peacekeeping in the wake of the end of the Cold War. The key security institutions in which the Federal Republic plays a role—the Atlantic Alliance, the European Union (EU) and the Western European Union (WEU) as well as the United Nations (UN) and the Organization for Security and Cooperation in Europe (OSCE)—had all embraced peacekeeping as a new and central mission for the post–Cold War period.

As Germans started to debate the future role of the Bundeswehr, the one issue that all the major political parties seemed to agree on was Bundeswehr participation in UN peacekeeping operations. Peacekeeping also seemed to resonate positively in both German elite and public opinion as an area where the country could and should assume a more active international role. Public opinion polls showed overwhelming public support for possible German participation in peacekeeping operations.[1] For some Germans, it seemed to represent the proper balance between the need for Germany to assume greater international responsibility and the desire to restrict the scope of Germany's future military role. This was, and in some ways continues to be, the primary prism through which much of the debate on the future of the Bundeswehr is filtered.

At the same time, it was also clear that the peacekeeping issue was part of a much broader political struggle over defining the future shape and scope of post–Cold War German foreign and security policy For some in the German political class, peacekeeping was but the first step in "normalizing" German foreign and security policy. A unified and fully sovereign Germany was to become a country with the same military rights and responsibilities as its key partners and allies. This was not only a matter of principle, but a practical matter of sustaining the vitality of those institutions to which Germany had entrusted its security, namely, the Atlantic Alliance and the European Union.

---

[1]See, for example, Ronald D. Asmus, *German Strategy and Public Opinion After the Wall 1990–1993*, Santa Monica, Calif.: RAND, MR-444-FNF/OSD/A/AF, 1994.

For the proponents of "normalization," it seemed apparent from the outset that the simplistic distinction often made in public between politically and morally acceptable peacekeeping and unacceptable combat operations—or what opponents called "war missions" (Kriegseinsätze)—was not sustainable intellectually, politically, or militarily. Intellectually, they argued that neat distinction between peacekeeping, peacemaking, and war-fighting often broke down in the real world, defying the neat and separate categories in which they were often discussed in German politics. Politically, they argued that for Germany to limit its future security role to the narrow category of peacekeeping ran the risk of not only isolating the country in both the EU and NATO, but undercutting the ability of those institutions to act in any meaningful way in the post–Cold War world.

For Germany to say that it would participate only in so-called "good" peacekeeping while leaving the more onerous task of peacemaking or war-fighting to its allies, they argued, combined moral arrogance and political impotence. Militarily, they argued that if and when German armed forces participated in such missions, they had to be flexible and prepared for changes that could take place on the ground. If Germany wanted to insure that institutions such as NATO, the EU/WEU, or the UN were effective in the future, they would have to participate in the full spectrum of new missions these institutions assumed and not try to carve out some special German role.

Opponents, in turn, argued that in reality "normalization" amounted to a "remilitarization" of German foreign policy in the post–Cold War world. In their eyes, there was not only no need for Germany to embark on such a course, but it was potentially dangerous. Not only could it unnecessarily draw Germany into conflicts and potential quagmires, often at the behest of Bonn's allies, it could also lead, they argued, to a shift to the right in German politics and the renationalization of German national security thinking. They accused the German government of using the peacekeeping issue as a wedge, essentially using "salami tactics" to dilute and eventually eliminate the restrictions on the use of the German armed forces. In the eyes of the most passionate critics, the broadening of the mission of the Bundeswehr was but a halfway house to a possible rebirth of a new form of German militarism. It was therefore necessary to draw the line—legally and politically—once and for all to prevent Germany from heading down this path.

As a result, the peacekeeping issue became a skirmish in a larger political drama over Germany's future strategic orientation and role in Europe and beyond. Arguments over how to define Germany's peacekeeping role generated political gridlock over how to interpret the country's constitution, a debate that was ultimately decided in the German Supreme Court in Karlsruhe in July 1994. While political parties bickered over the differences between peacekeeping and peacemaking and where Bonn should or should not draw the line for its future engagement, the ruling coalition, nevertheless, started to create facts on the ground by involving German troops in a variety of UN missions beyond Germany's borders ranging from Iraq, Cambodia, and Bosnia to Somalia, thereby breaking down the political and psychological barriers against a German military role overseas.

Although much of the initial German enthusiasm for peacekeeping has since been tempered by a growing realization of the difficulties and costs involved, peacekeeping remains at the center of the German debate for two simple reasons. First, the July 1994 German Supreme Court decision laid to rest any questions about constitutional constraints restricting a German peacekeeping role. The German government has since designed its plans to restructure the German armed forces to create a significant capability appropriate for future peacekeeping and other missions. Politicians have since taken up the issues of criteria and the modalities of parliamentary approval for peacekeeping missions.

In short, with many of the official constraints on the use of the German armed forces removed, it is only a matter of time until Germany becomes more involved in peace support operations. The shift became apparent in late 1994 when Bonn faced the issue of whether it would participate in plans for the evacuation of United Nations Protection Force (UNPROFOR) forces from the former Yugoslavia. Only a few years earlier, many German politicians had excluded, in principle, any German military participation in the former Yugoslavia. Moreover, when NATO AWACS planes were used to monitor the UN-sanctioned embargo against Serbia, the issue of German participation in those flights created a coalition crisis within the German government. By late 1994, Bonn's answer was a yes, albeit a qualified yes, underscoring just how far the German debate had moved.[2]

Second, the peacekeeping issue remains an important microcosm of the much broader debate over how a unified Germany should define its future security and role. It remains the primary vehicle through which Germans are seeking to sort out definitions of national interests, criteria for the use of force, modalities of parliamentary approval, etc. It has forced the German political class and public to start thinking about and debating these issues. As a result, Germany is starting to experience the kinds of debates too familiar to an American reader—e.g., foreign and defense ministers disagreeing in public about the use of force, disputes over the proper balance of authority between the executive and legislative branches. How these core political issues are resolved will determine just how active a peacekeeping role Germany will play.

This report examines the evolution of the German peacekeeping debate. It examines the political and military stepping stones in this debate, above all key decisions and plans for restructuring the Bundeswehr for new peacekeeping and other missions. It also examines several key unanswered questions in the German debate, including the issue of public support for future peace support operations.

---

[2]On December 21, 1994, the German government announced that it would, in principle, be ready to provide German forces if a NATO evacuation of UNPROFOR forces proved necessary. Bonn qualified its yes, however, by noting that it would be willing to provide logistical assistance and combat air cover but that no German ground combat troops would participate in such an operation. While the Social Democratic opposition voiced doubts about the participation of German Tornado fighter bombers, coalition leaders noted that the only requirement for parliamentary approval was a simple majority. See the *Frankfurter Allgemeine Zeitung*, December 22, 1994. On February 22, 1995, the German cabinet officially approved German participation in such an evacuation. See *Frankfurter Allgemeine Zeitung*, February 23, 1995.

Chapter Two

GERMANY'S NEW GEOPOLITICS

The peacekeeping issue is intertwined with the broader debate over how to define the interests and responsibilities of a unified Germany in the post–Cold War era. The outcome of this broader debate will define the when, where, and how of Germany's future peacekeeping role. The key components of this debate have been, first, the attempt to define Germany's vital interest in a radically altered European strategic landscape. In a sense, this is the debate over the where and when of future German participation in peacekeeping missions.

The German debate has largely focused on Europe and the need to insulate Germany from potential new instability, above all in the East. As the initial euphoria following the collapse of communism has worn off, Germans have become increasingly aware of the new risks and vulnerabilities inherent in Europe's new strategic landscape. While a unified Germany is, in many ways, Europe's most powerful country, it has also (again) inherited the enduring dilemmas rooted in geography and geopolitics, or what German geopoliticians and historians have termed the Mittellage or "the position in the middle" on an unstable continent.

A unified Germany today, however, once again occupies its historical position at Europe's crossroads, the place where cultures and ideologies of the West and East have clashed, commingled, and competed with one another. The country's destiny and fate have never been solely determined by events within its borders, but rather by the interaction of those events with trends further West and East. To be stronger than any of its individual neighbors, yet not strong enough to dominate them should they coalesce in a coalition against it, has been Germany's enduring strategic dilemma throughout history. It is the "country in the middle" playing the role of bridge builder in a very unbalanced Europe—politically, economically, and militarily.[1]

The inability of German statesmen to manage the multiple challenges of the Mittellage is seen by many historians as a primary cause for a decades-long pattern of geopolitical instability in Central Europe and ultimately for German attempts to try to dominate the region and a strategic orientation that produced two world wars. It was Konrad Adenauer's determination to break out of the trap of the Mittellage that led him to push for the deep integration of the new West German state into the West to prevent a future Germany from again engaging in such geopolitical jockeying.[2]

For this generation of German leaders, the answer to Germany's dilemma is to insure the country's integration into the West, and to try to extend those structures to the East to insulate Germany from new instability, a resurgence of nationalism, and geopolitical competition on the continent. Chancellor Helmut Kohl has repeatedly termed the issue of European integration a question of "war and peace" for Europe.[3] Similarly, the controversial "Schäuble paper" issued by the Christian Democratic Union (CDU) in the fall of 1994 calling for a multispeed Europe justified this step by pointing to Germany's Mittellage dilemma and the need to deepen integration to counter a resurgence of destabilizing geopolitical dynamics in European politics.[4] Finally, German Defense Minister Volker Rühe's campaign to expand NATO eastward to anchor and shield the new

---

[1]As German President Richard von Weizsäcker noted in April 1992: "Already the first two years after the fall of the Berlin Wall have been enough to drastically show us the kinds of problems this *Mittellage* in Europe brings with it, a *Mittellage* that has characterized Germany's position since the end of the Holy Roman Empire and which led us into two world wars after 1914." See Richard von Weizsäcker, "Maastricht als historische Chance," *Frankfurter Allgemeine Zeitung*, April 13, 1992.

[2]See, for example, Hans-Peter Schwarz, *Adenauer: Der Aufstieg: 1876–1952* (Stuttgart: Deutsche Verlags-Anstalt, 1986).

[3]See Kohl's Bundestag speech in *Das Parlament*, November 26, 1993, p. 2.

[4]See Josef Joffe's interview with Wolfgang Schäuble in *Süddeutsche Zeitung*, September 12, 1994, p. 9.

fragile democracies of East-Central Europe has been driven by a similar set of concerns.[5]

In short, Germany's response has been to turn to its key allies, and those Western institutions that have guaranteed German security in the post-war period—the EU and NATO—and to reshape them to meet Germany's new needs, above all in the East. As a result, Germany has become the driving force in European politics behind calls for the expansion of both the EU and NATO to include the countries of East-Central Europe to guard against new instability arising on Germany's eastern flank while, at the same time, trying to establish a new cooperative set of relations with Russia and the successor states of the Soviet Union.

The most vocal and articulate proponent of NATO and EU expansion has been German Defense Minister Volker Rühe. Rühe represents a new breed of younger, more assertive German politicians who have spoken more openly and candidly about Germany's interests and the need for Germany to step out of its old Cold War niche on foreign and security policy issues. For many years he has led the effort within the CDU to establish a higher profile on these issues. Rühe has used the relative weakness of Genscher's successor as foreign minister, Klaus Kinkel, to try to establish a higher profile for the Ministry of Defense and for himself as a key figure on broader strategic issues. His views have sparked controversy within the coalition, as well as his own party, and his ambition has led him to clash at times with his own chancellor.

While Rühe remains controversial, many of the positions he has staked out have become mainstream views in German politics. To be sure, the issues of sequence and modalities between EU and NATO expansion remain contentious, as does the issue of how one should attempt to construct a new "strategic partnership" with Russia. Such differences notwithstanding, there is a growing consensus within the mainstream German political parties that Germany has the greatest interest in a relatively rapid expansion of both NATO and the EU to East-Central Europe. Speaking in the Bundestag debate following the NATO summit, Defense Minister Rühe summed up what was

---

[5]See Volker Rühe, "Shaping Euro-Atlantic Policies: A Grand Strategy for a New Era," *Survival*, Summer 1993, pp. 135–142.

becoming a near consensus position in German politics when he stated:

> The opening of the Alliance to the East is in our vital interests. One does not have to be a strategic genius to understand this. I have often been surprised how little our debate on this issue has been guided by a clear analysis of German interests. A border of stability and security—unstable east of us but stable here, prosperity this side of the border, poverty on the other—such a situation is not sustainable in the long run. It is for this reason that Germany's eastern border cannot be the eastern border of NATO and the European Union. Either we will export stability or we will end up importing instability.[6]

At the same time, the German political class is increasingly realizing that such institutions will move in this direction only if Germany emerges from the geopolitical niche it occupied during the Cold War and becomes a more active player in determining the future gestalt of Europe. Furthermore, Germany has also sought to define a new role through the United Nations. Although concern over growing instability in and around Europe has increasingly refocused German diplomacy on problems closer to home, Bonn has continued to place a top priority on strengthening the United Nations, becoming increasingly engaged in a range of peacekeeping missions. UN Secretary General Boutros Boutros-Ghali has strongly and publicly encouraged Germany to become more active in UN operations. Germany has also announced its interest in a seat on the UN Security Council.[7]

The second component of this debate has revolved around the appropriate instruments for future German security policy, above all the use of military force. This is the "how" of peacekeeping. German Defense Minister Volker Rühe has coined the phrase "culture of reticence" to describe the strategic culture of the pre-unification Federal Republic. What he was referring to was the reluctance of

---

[6]See Rühe's Bundestag speech reprinted in *Das Parlament*, No. 3, January 21, 1994.

[7]See Wolfgang Wagner, "Der ständige Sitz im Sicherheitsrat," *Europa-Archiv*, No. 19/1993, pp. 533–540. Also Karl Kaiser, "Die ständige Mitgliedschaft im Sicherheitsrat," *Europa-Archiv*, No. 19/1993, pp. 541–552.

Germans to think in terms of the use of force for much of the post-war period for reasons rooted in German history.

When the Federal Republic was created in 1949, it was devoid of any military instruments. When the decision was made to rearm the Federal Republic in the mid-1950s, Germany was not being rehabilitated as a power where armed forces were a "normal" instrument of statecraft; rather, the German military contribution was an integrated part of a broader U.S.-led effort to contain Soviet expansionism. The full integration of German armed forces into NATO command structures and the lack of any national military command structure in peacetime or for missions other than territorial defense underscored the special and limited nature of Germany's military contribution.

Within the Federal Republic itself, NATO was seen by Germans as a political instrument to organize allied support for the defense of German territory and interests. Almost no thought was given to the possibility that German forces might be called upon to assist another member of the alliance. In Germany it became conventional wisdom that no one wanted to see Germany ever again develop a major military role outside territorial defense. Such a view was willingly embraced in a country with its own war trauma and the discredited legacy of the use of military force to achieve political purposes rooted in the excesses of National Socialism and its glorification of the cult of war and power politics.

While Germans were willing to recognize the legitimacy of military force as a necessary instrument for containing Soviet power, they frequently had problems with the notion that responsible democracies could and should, under certain circumstances, rely on military force to preserve stability or to uphold principles of international law. The destruction of Germany during the Second World War, coupled with the realization that a future military conflict in Central Europe between NATO and the Warsaw Pact would have devastating consequences for both German states, reinforced the conviction that German security policy had to be aimed at deterring war on Germany's borders and that no other political goals could be achieved through the use of force.

It became increasingly fashionable in Germany to argue that Germans had learned the lessons of history and that German policy should aim to create a world where force was no longer a legitimate tool to achieve desired political goals. This trend seemed to be reinforced by generational change and the emergence of the so-called "successor generation" in German politics.[8] In the mid-1980s the German historian Hans-Peter Schwarz captured this transformation in German attitudes toward power from Hitler to the Federal Republic in a book entitled *The Tamed Germans,* in which he argued that whereas Germans had previously been preoccupied with power politics, they had now developed an "obliviousness to power" that helped explain the strength of the German peace movement and the seeming inability of many Germans to think in categories of geopolitics and military power.[9]

The end of the Cold War initially seemed to reinforce the view that military power was passé. The dominant intellectual fashion in much of the Western world was to pronounce that in a post–Cold War order, military power was increasingly outdated and was being supplanted by economic might in a new world order in which countries such as Germany and Japan would reign supreme. German academics and politicians, especially among German Social Democrats, embraced notions of Germany as a "civilian power" that could eschew traditional military power and turn its "culture of reticence" into a political bonus.[10]

A more active German military role, they argued, was not only not necessary but potentially dangerous. It was unnecessary because a new age of cooperative security was dawning and the need for and utility of military power was diminishing. It was dangerous, they suggested, because it could prove to be a slippery slope that could again prove to be a halfway house for the "militarization" and eventual renationalization of German national security policy. Instead, they argued that Germany should concentrate on the attributes of

---

[8]See Stephen F. Szabo (ed.), *The Successor Generation: International Perspectives of Postwar Europeans* (Boston: Buttersworth, 1983).

[9]See Hans-Peter Schwarz, *Die gezähmten Deutschen. Von der Machtbesessenheit zur Machtvergessenheit* (Stuttgart: Deutsche Verlags-Anstalt, 1985).

[10]See Hanns W. Maull, "Zivilmacht Bundesrepublik Deutschland. Vierzehn Thesen für eine neue deutsche Aussenpolitik," *Europa Archiv,* No. 10, 1992, pp. 269–278.

what Joe Nye once called "soft power"—economic and financial influence, culture, ecology, etc. Having learned the lessons of militarism in two world wars, Germany, they argued, should leave the fighting of wars to others, practice geopolitical abstinence, and lead by example.[11]

Other voices, first and foremost the German government, vehemently rejected such views as potentially leading to a strategic nightmare for Germany. Instead, they insisted that the time had finally come for Germany to become a "normal" power and to shed both the political and psychological constraints that had shackled the security and defense policy of the Federal Republic during the Cold War. This had nothing to do with German megalomania, they insisted, but reflected the sober realization that to do otherwise would mean creating some sort of special German pacifistic mission that would isolate Germany internationally. If Germany were unwilling or unable to undertake the same risks and responsibilities as its allies, they insisted, German policy would contribute to the weakening and ultimate demise of both the EU and NATO. This, in turn, would rekindle the renationalization of European politics.

Preventing that, government officials stated, was an overriding German interest. The danger of renationalization, they argued, could best be contained by Germany assuming a more active strategic role that would insure that those institutions remained vital and dealt with the key strategic issues of the day, including Germany's core concerns and interests.[12] While reluctant to discuss the issue in public, German government officials knew that the most likely challenges to future European security all lay beyond NATO's borders—in the Persian Gulf, Northern Africa, and the Mediterranean as well as in the Balkans—and that Bonn's key allies expected more than German participation in traditional consensual peacekeeping.

---

[11]See, for example, Peter Glotz, *Die falsche Normalisierung. Essays* (Frankfurt a.M.: Suhrkamp Verlag, 1994).

[12]The need for Germany to assume this role to maintain the vitality of European integration and the Atlantic Alliance has been a constant theme in the speeches of German Defense Minster Volker Rühe. See, for example, Volker Rühe, *Deutschlands Verantwortung* (Berlin: Ullstein Verlag, 1994).

The issue at the heart of this debate crystallized around the notion of Germany's "culture of reticence"—a phrase coined by the German defense minister to characterize post-war Germany's aversion to the use of force and the old division of labor within the West whereby Germany's military role was circumscribed to territorial defense. Rühe, while acknowledging the historical reasons for this culture of reticence and the resonance it evoked in some circles of elite and public opinion, nevertheless made it clear that a unified Germany had to move beyond such a stance. Whereas Rühe portrayed the "culture of reticence" as an obstacle to be transcended, many opponents saw it as a badge of courage and proof of German moral superiority that a unified Germany had to preserve.

Real world events soon overtook what initially seemed to be a rather academic debate. The Gulf War destroyed the illusion that all conflicts could be resolved through peaceful means and the war in the former Yugoslavia shattered the belief that war had been banned from the European continent. Both also underscored the point that the expectations of Germany's allies and partners had changed, and that Germany's key allies in the EU, NATO, and the United Nations all expected Germany to assume a greater military role. The combined impact of these factors served as a catalyst for a profound process of rethinking assumptions about the type of world German foreign policy will be confronted with in the future and questioning whether Germany is equipped with the proper strategic mindset and policy instruments.[13]

It was against this backdrop that the major political battle over the future of German security policy and strategy took place. The most visible venue for this battle was the struggle over how to interpret the

---

[13]In the words of the German writer Peter Schneider at the time: "Although it still remains unclear whether the allied troops successfully achieved a total blackout over Saddam's armies, what is certain is that Germany's radar screen went blank following the events of August 1990. The political and moral prism through which we Germans viewed the world suddenly shattered." See Peter Schneider, "Das falsche gute Gewissen der Friedensbewegung," *Frankfurter Allgemeine Zeitung,* April 19, 1991. See also Ronald D. Asmus, *Germany After the Gulf War,* Santa Monica, Calif.: RAND, N-3391-AF, 1992. On the changing expectation of Germany's allies, see Ronald D. Asmus, "Fragen unter Freunden," *Die Zeit,* February 15, 1991. For the inside story on Bonn's real contribution to the Gulf War effort, see Michael J. Inacker, *Unter Ausschluss der Öffentlichkeit. Die Deutschen in der Golfallianz* (Bonn: Bouvier Verlag, 1991).

German constitution. The origins of this story can be traced back to the mid-1970s. Although the Bundeswehr's role had been largely limited to territorial defense, the Federal Republic's political and economic rehabilitation had led to occasional feelers as to whether Bonn would contribute to UN peacekeeping or other military operations. German Chancellor Helmut Schmidt and Foreign Minister Hans-Dietrich Genscher opposed such military involvement for several reasons. In addition to the issue of how to interpret the constitution, they were concerned that, in light of the East-West dimension and escalatory potential of many potential crises outside of Europe, German military involvement could quickly reverberate into Central Europe, thereby endangering German detente policy. Germany's division was also seen as leaving Bonn especially vulnerable to Soviet pressure.[14]

Genscher and the Foreign Office, however, subsequently publicly interpreted the German constitution as being the reason why Bonn opposed such military involvement, thereby helping to establish the view that the deployment of German troops beyond German soil was unconstitutional. Although defense ministry officials tried to force the Foreign Office to clarify the issue, the issue remained unresolved within the Bonn bureaucracy. Successive German governments chose to continue to sweep the issue under the rug and to interpret

---

[14]Vice Admiral Ulrich Weisser would subsequently confirm this German concern in a book authored shortly before he became head of Rühe's Policy and Planning Staff in the German MoD when he wrote: "In addition to the constitution, two main arguments were used against involving Germans in efforts to preserve international law and order in other parts of the world, above all against Germany making available its military forces. First, in Bonn one saw—not entirely without justification—that a German participation in resolving conflicts in other parts of the world under the conditions of the East-West conflict also contained the danger that a conflict that appeared at first glance to be regional could escalate into a direct confrontation [on German soil]. This danger was especially marked in the German view after the United States introduced the strategic axiom of horizontal escalation into its national strategy. It thereby created the option of retaliating on another flank—thereby quite consciously viewing the alliance as an instrument for regional conflict resolution. This argument is void with the resolution of the East-West conflict. The second German reservation lay in our own critical view of the burdens of German history. The development of Germany into a stable democracy, a respected member of the world community, a global economic power, and the promoter of a European peace order has led to a situation where Germany will now be allowed to return to normality. Trust in Germany is in the meantime often greater outside Germany than inside of the country. This second reservation has also become obsolete." See Ulrich Weisser, *NATO Ohne Feindbild* (Bonn: Bouvier Verlag, 1992), p. 29.

the constitution as limiting the mission of the German armed forces to national self-defense. In the late 1980s, several German conservatives, including CDU Defense Minister Rupert Scholz, himself a well-known expert on the German constitution, publicly challenged Genscher's view on this but the issue went unresolved, only to become a hot-button political issue as a result of the Gulf War and the peacekeeping issue.

Chapter Three

REASSESSING GERMAN STRATEGY

It was against this backdrop that a broader political drama has taken place in German politics in which the peacekeeping issue was a central figure. The drama was over the scope and content of future German security policy. The peacekeeping debate was a central figure in this drama, first, because of the merits of the issue and the recognized need across the political spectrum to strengthen the UN and conflict prevention policies; and, second, because it became the venue through which this broader struggle over Germany's future orientation would be waged. If the opponents to Germany's assuming a more active military role could draw the line at consensual peacekeeping missions, then any discussion of Germany's ultimately assuming other combat missions was clearly moot. For the proponents of "normalization," it was an issue that could be used to set the terms of reference for a broader debate over Germany's interests and role in post–Cold War Europe as well as to provide political cover for what would clearly be a major reorientation for the German armed forces that would require time.

As a result, the peacekeeping issue was debated at a time and in a context when some of the core assumptions underlying past German foreign and defense policy were being revisited. Moreover, following the surprise resignation of Hans-Dietrich Genscher as foreign minister in early 1993, the political and intellectual impetus in this debate started to shift to the defense ministry, where Volker Rühe and his closest aides had assumed power and soon launched a major effort to build a new political and conceptual foundation for future German strategy and the German armed forces. Whereas Genscher and the Foreign Office had traditionally dominated security and foreign policy, Rühe was now clearly determined to establish a greater role for himself and the defense ministry in shaping German policy and strategy in the post–Cold War world.

Although Rühe's outspoken views on expanding NATO have elicited controversy, it is important to note that his overall efforts to transform German security policy, military strategy, and the role of the Bundeswehr have largely enjoyed the chancellor's support. To be sure, the issue of the future role of the Bundeswehr beyond German borders has also been controversial. There have been major differences within the ruling coalition as well as within the Bundestag on Germany's future military role. The political battles of past years notwithstanding, the CDU-led government has clarified the legal mandate of the Bundeswehr, established the political parameters for future Bundeswehr operations, embraced a new conceptual framework, initiated a restructuring process for the German armed forces, and reached agreement on future funding for the years ahead. While key questions still need to be resolved, this underscores just how far Germany has moved in a relatively short period of time.

This saga can perhaps best be told by looking at the attempts of the German government, above all the Minister of Defense, to establish a new political and strategic assessment of German interests and rationale for the Bundeswehr and to restructure the German armed forces accordingly. The terms of this new debate were largely set by a small group of senior officials in and around Rühe in the German MoD. Three arguments were crucial. The first was a new assessment of Europe's strategic landscape and the role of Germany in it, and the implications for Germany's armed forces. A unified Germany found itself in a paradoxical situation. On the one hand, it was the greatest beneficiary of the end of the Cold War in security terms. It was now surrounded by friendly and largely weaker countries, and was no longer within the strategic reach of forces capable of launching a major offensive against German territory.

At the same time, the future risks to Germany had to be viewed from the viewpoint of broader European stability and the threats that could emerge on Europe's periphery and spread back to the center of the continent.[1] Senior German MoD officials noted the importance not only to Germany of developments in Eastern Europe and Russia, but of the need to include new factors in the German strategic calculus—e.g., Germany's access to strategic raw materials, the need to prevent proliferation, and challenges that could face German interests in places such as Northern Africa or the Middle East. Old Cold War concepts of "in" and "out of area," they insisted, no longer made strategic sense in a new Europe. As one senior German Foreign Office representative put it in an interview with this author in the fall of 1991, the concept of "out of area is an anachronism of the Cold War. All the new threats to and in Europe are 'out of area.' For Germany what happens in and to Poland is far more important than events on the Iberian peninsula."

Defense Minister Rühe repeatedly argued that although the direct military threat to German soil had evaporated, Germany's Mittellage meant that it had a vital interest in insuring stability on Europe's flanks and periphery. In addition to the uncertainties concerning Russia's future, the dangers of rising nationalism, disintegration, and emerging new conflicts à la Bosnia posed a threat to important German interests. Given its geographic position, Germany had a stronger interest than almost all of its key allies in insuring such regional stability.[2] As General Klaus Naumann subsequently put it, Germany's participation in peacekeeping and crisis management operations offers "a chance to keep wars away from our territory."[3]

Senior German defense officials sought to capture the shift in German strategy by speaking of Germany moving from being an "importer" to becoming an "exporter" of security, or, alternatively, of Germany shifting from a consumer of security to a producer thereof in the post–Cold War era. In the spring of 1992, the senior leadership of the Bundeswehr started to develop a new and broader political and strategic rationale for the German armed forces. Penned by

---

[1]See "Militärpolitische und Militärstrategische Grundlagen und Konzeptionelle Grundrichtung der Neugestaltung der Bundeswehr," author's private copy.

[2]For the evolution of Rühe's thinking, see his speeches in Volker Rühe, *Bundeswehr. Sicherheitspolitik und Streitkräfte im Wandel* (Berlin: Verlag E. S. Mittler und Sohn, 1993).

[3]See Klaus Naumann, "German Security Policy and Future Tasks of the Bundeswehr," *Defense and International Security*, December 1994, p. 12.

General Klaus Naumann, the so-called "Naumann Paper" sought to lay out a strategic planning framework for the German armed forces for the period after 1995—i.e., after the completion of the withdrawal of the forces of the former USSR from German soil—along such lines.

The second key argument revolved around the implications of Germany's future military role for the reform of the Atlantic Alliance and the European integration process. Bonn officials repeatedly emphasized that expectations regarding Germany's future contribution had changed. They insisted that Germany, more than any other member of NATO, has a strong interest in seeing the Alliance move in the direction of extending security beyond its traditional borders. For Germany not to participate in such efforts to revamp NATO as well as the WEU to meet Europe's new strategic challenges would both marginalize Germany within these institutions, condemning it to a second-class status, and ultimately contribute to their growing ineffectiveness and possible downfall.

In particular, senior German defense officials pointed to the danger that were Germany not to participate in future non–Article 5 missions, it might find itself increasingly out of step with the United States strategically, especially with the evolving mission of U.S. forces in Germany. This, they argued, could lead to strategic estrangement between the two countries, something Bonn desperately wanted to avoid. What was at stake, they insisted, was the future predictability and effectiveness of German foreign and security policy. As Defense Minister Rühe put it in a meeting with senior military leaders in the fall of 1993, Germany was paying a price for the unresolved debate over the future role of the German armed forces. In his words:

> [This debate] limits our ability to have a German foreign and defense policy. It is damaging our credibility and our image. There will never be a common foreign and defense policy, nor a European Defense nor an effective crisis management policy in the Alliance so long as Germany must regularly note its reservations regarding the using of force.

> This endless constitutional debate is restricting the process of European integration which is essential for us. It is damaging the trans-Atlantic relationship which is the very foundation of our secu-

rity. And it endangers the reform of NATO which urgently must face new challenges. This discussion must be stopped.[4]

The third argument centered on the implications of this analysis for the Bundeswehr. Having been built during the Cold War, the Bundeswehr was prepared and equipped for deterring or fighting a major ground war in Central Europe against a powerful enemy. It was specifically designed to defend German territory, and largely lacked the logistics and C3I elements required to give it projection capabilities. As a result, it was poorly equipped—psychologically, logistically, in terms of force posture and training—for dealing with any of the new challenges likely to face Germany and Europe in the years ahead. While Bonn, of course, had to remain concerned about the resurgence of an expansionist Russia, this threat was no longer Germany's sole or even main security concern, senior German defense officials argued.

Although a renewed Russian threat could pose the most serious strategic challenge to German interests, it was not the most likely. Rather, the real challenge was to maintain those core capabilities essential for the European balance of power and to guard against a new Russian threat, but also to revamp the Bundeswehr for the spectrum of non–Article 5 missions as well, ranging from peacekeeping to crisis management. In the words of Vice Admiral Ulrich Weisser, head of Policy and Planning in the German Ministry of Defense:

> One must differentiate between the most dangerous and the most likely dimensions of future conflicts. Europe's central region still contains certain strategic risks but the probability for conflict is small and only conceivable following a basic shift in the political constellation. In the eastern part of the continent and on the periphery of Europe, above all on its southern flank, the probability of conflict is considerably higher, but the direct dimension of the threat to us is smaller. A future European security and military structure must take both categories of risk into account and,

---

[4]See Rühe's speech before the annual Kommandeurtagung in Mainz in October 1993 entitled "Deutsche Sicherheitspolitik vor neuen Aufgaben," *Bulletin*, No. 83, October 8, 1993.

moreover, be directed toward the new elements in this spectrum of threats.[5]

Starting in early 1992, the German government took a series of steps designed to initiate the transformation of the Bundeswehr along these lines. In February 1992, the German government clarified that the Bundeswehr's mission was not limited to the defense of German territory but that it included in-region or what Rühe called "extended defense" within NATO's borders—i.e., that the Bundeswehr could be deployed beyond Germany in both combat and noncombat roles (e.g., Turkey).   Then German Defense Minister Gerhard Stoltenberg emphasized that this new law would allow German forces to participate in NATO's planned Rapid Reaction Force, but that Bundeswehr participation in peacekeeping or other missions under UN auspices would require a further clarification of the German constitution.[6]

This modest step was nonetheless considered a breakthrough. Not only had it been supported by then Foreign Minister Hans-Dietrich Genscher, who had traditionally opposed any widening of the Bundeswehr's mandate, but it gave an early green light for the Bundeswehr leadership to start both planning and developing the capabilities for the reorientation of the Bundeswehr from territorial defense to in-region defense. As one high-ranking German MoD official nevertheless told the author at the time: "This law is a breakthrough. It allows the Bundeswehr to start developing the prerequisites to operate in, for example, Turkey. If we can fight in Turkey, then we have the capability to go a lot of places if and when the political parameters of this debate change."

In November 1992, the new German Defense Minister Volker Rühe issued a new Defense Policy Guidance (DPG) for the German armed forces. This was the first official attempt to clarify German interests in the post–Cold War world and the implications for German defense planning. The emphasis was on Germany's interests beyond its borders and the German stake in the UN and in seeing NATO develop

---

[5]See Weisser, op cit., p. 153.

[6]See Stoltenberg's press statement, *BMVg, Presse Mitteilung No. XXIX/13*, February 19, 1992.

adequate crisis management capabilities for dealing with conflict in and around Europe. It embraced the traditional goals of maintaining the Atlantic Alliance, nuclear deterrence, as well as a new "partnership among equals" between the United States and Europe. Although developments in Russia are still the most serious possible threat to German security, the DPG also emphasized the dangers of proliferation and regional conflict in Europe and on the periphery leading to a destabilization of the continent. Such threats, it argued, "must be met with preventive action at the place of their origin and before they have a chance to escalate."

NATO, according to the German DPG, has a role of projecting stability throughout Europe and must, therefore, increasingly reflect these broader strategic trends. "NATO must develop more relevance for crises and conflicts in an expanded geographic area in order to be an anchor of stability for all of Europe," including opening itself to the East. The German Bundeswehr was seen as being best prepared for the least likely threat—i.e., a resurgent Russia—and poorly prepared for the array of new crises that could emerge in the future affecting German interests. The DPG pointed to the challenge of expanding the operational and geographic orientation of the Bundeswehr at a time when it is simultaneously completing unification of the German armed forces, implementing deep cuts in the overall size of the force, and facing very deep budget cuts. It also called for the creation of two battalions for peacekeeping by October 1, 1993.[7]

The DPG was followed by the issuing of the German White Paper in April 1994. The first German White Paper issued since the mid-1970s, this document presented the German government's (i.e., not only the German MoD's) attempt to lay out the political and strategic rationale for a new German security and defense policy in the post–Cold War era. In spirit and philosophy, it followed along the lines of the DPG, although the inter-agency process did lead to a softening of some of the language and the specifics. The White Paper nevertheless did reaffirm the overall thrust of Rühe's efforts at a new strategic assessment of the risks and vulnerabilities that Germany

---

[7]See *Verteidigungspolitische Richtlinien* (Bonn: Ministry of Defense, November 1992). See also Dieter Mahnke, "Wandel im Wandel: Bundeswehr und europäische Sicherheit," *Das Parlament, Aus Politik und Zeitgeschichte,* B 15-16, April 9, 1993, pp. 40–46.

faced in the new Europe and the need to transform the Bundeswehr into a force capable of meeting a broad spectrum of new missions and threats. The growing importance of the UN and peacekeeping in German policy was reflected in the fact that a separate section in the White Paper is devoted to Germany's growing military involvement in UN activities since 1991.

The latter underscored another aspect in the Bonn government's strategy to develop peacekeeping capabilities since 1990. While the political debate continued unabated over how to interpret the constitution, the government went ahead and involved the Bundeswehr in a growing number of UN operations—UNAMIC and UNTAC in Cambodia, mine clearing in the Arabian Gulf, UNSCOM in Iraq, the Kurdish relief operation, UNOSOM-II in Somalia—and a variety of relief missions in the former Yugoslavia—e.g., the Sarajevo airlift, airdrops over eastern Bosnia, monitoring of the flight ban over Bosnia-Hercegovina, and the monitoring of the Adriatic embargo. By doing so, the ruling coalition in Bonn was trying to push the envelope and not only outmaneuver the parliamentary opposition but also create political and psychological facts that would accustom the German public to the German armed forces participating in such activities.

Pushing the envelope also brought the political issue of how to interpret the German constitution to a head in the German parliament. The dispute over this issue led to a series of complicated political and legal maneuvers that even the most experienced viewers of the German political scene were hard pressed to interpret and explain, eventually catalyzing three separate suits filed against the German government by the parliamentary opposition including, in one case, the Free Democratic Party (FDP) as a member of the ruling coalition. The Social Democratic Party (SPD) opposition increasingly accused the Bonn government of the "remilitarization" of German foreign policy, insisting that the role of the Bundeswehr should be strictly limited to traditional consensual peacekeeping missions under a clear UN mandate. The ruling coalition, in contrast, insisted that the Bundeswehr had to be able to participate in the full range of peace support and other non–Article 5 missions. However, there were differences within the coalition as to whether a constitutional amendment was required. The German Foreign Office, led by Foreign Minister and FDP Chairman Klaus Kinkel, insisted that the government amend the constitution to clarify any ambiguities concerning the role of the Bundeswehr. Chancellor Helmut Kohl's Christian Democrats, on the other hand, insisted that there was no need for a constitutional amendment, which would have required a two-thirds vote in the Bundestag.

Following failed efforts to reach a compromise in parliament, the issue was eventually taken to the German Supreme Court in Karlsruhe. In a case that at times confused even long-standing observers of the German political scene, the German Supreme Court was called upon to rule in three different cases touching upon the issue of peacekeeping and the role of the Bundeswehr in out-of-area operations. In August 1992, the opposition SPD had filed suit against the participation of a German frigate in the Adriatic embargo against Serbia and Montenegro. In April 1993, the SPD—this time in conjunction with the ruling FDP—filed suit against the participation of Germans troops in AWACS flights over Hungary; and in May 1993, the SPD also filed suit against the participation of the Bundeswehr in Somalia.

Unlike the Japanese constitution, the German Basic Law contains no explicit references to the role of the German armed forces. The controversy revolved around how to interpret Articles 24, 59, and 87. Article 24 allows the Federal Republic to abandon parts of its sovereignty in joining a collective security system; Article 59 regulates parliamentary approval of treaty matters; and Article 87 refers to the creation of armed forces for "the purpose of defense." As a result, the German Supreme Court was essentially asked to rule on three issues. What were the normal tasks of a collective security system? What kind of parliamentary approval was the executive branch required to seek before German armed forces could be engaged in such operations? How should the phrase "for the purpose of defense" be interpreted?

In a nutshell, the government argued that decision on the use of armed force should be confined to the executive branch, that tasks of a system of collective security made no distinction between the kinds of military operations armed forces might be involved in, and that the intent of the wording of Article 87 had not been to limit the role of the German armed forces. The opposition, on the other hand, essentially argued that missions going beyond traditional peacekeeping were not defensive, that the treaty obligations of the Federal

Republic under the Washington and Brussels Treaties were being qualitatively altered (and therefore required a new vote in the Bundestag), and that the government had violated the constitution by not seeking the necessary parliamentary approval for Bundeswehr participation in these new missions.[8]

On July 12, 1994, the German Supreme Court ruled that the German constitution empowered Bonn to join a collective security system and to assume the "tasks typically associated" with such a system regarding the use of the German armed forces. In short, it ruled that there are no constitutional limits on the kinds of missions the Bundeswehr can engage in. The hotly debated question of combat vs. noncombat missions was left to the decisionmaking authority of the German government. At the same time, the court also ruled that it was essential for the government to seek parliamentary approval for any deployment of German troops for purposes other than the defense of German territory on a case-by-case basis. A simple majority is sufficient to authorize all types of operations. Moreover, the court also explicitly stated that the German government was free to act without parliamentary consent in an emergency.[9]

To be sure, the court's ruling did not resolve all issues completely. It did not, for example, clarify the issue of exactly what kind of mandate was required for future operations. Similarly, the modalities of seeking parliamentary approval were left to the executive and legislative branches to sort out. The judges split on the issue of whether the adoption of new missions constituted a qualitative change in the character and substance of the Federal Republic's commitments under the Washington and Brussels Treaties. They suggested that this issue could arise again depending on how far NATO and the WEU move in this direction in the future.[10]   Such important caveats

---

[8]For the official statements of Foreign Minister Klaus Kinkel and Defense Minister Volker Rühe before the court, see *Bulletin*, No. 35, April 22, 1994.

[9]For further details, see the court's ruling entitled *Leitansätze zum Urteil des Zweiten Senats*, July 12, 1994, author's private copy.

[10]The possibility that the SPD might again return to the legal arguments over the issue of mandate or the threshhold at which the tasks of Germany's treaty obligations in NATO or the WEU change sufficiently to justify a treaty amendment was hinted at in an article by the SPD's lead lawyer in the case. See Michael Bothe, "Rätsel aus Karlsruhe," *Der Spiegel*, July 25, 1994.

notwithstanding, one thing was clear. The legal question mark over whether German troops can go "out of area" and participate in non–Article 5 missions, including the full range of peace support operations, had been lifted.[11]

---

[11]For reactions to the court's decision, see the stenographic report of the Bundestag debate of July 22, 1994, above all the speeches of Foreign Minister Klaus Kinkel, Defense Minister Volker Rühe, as well as those of SPD leader Rudolf Scharping and SPD foreign policy spokesman Karsten Voigt. See *Deutscher Bundestag, Stenographischer Bericht der 240 Sitzung,* July 22, 1994, author's private copy.

Chapter Four

PEACEKEEPING: NOT WHETHER, BUT WHEN AND HOW

The German Supreme Court decision of July 1994 was a watershed in the debate over the Bundeswehr's future and future peacekeeping missions. The question of the Bundeswehr participation in the full spectrum of non–Article 5 missions was transformed from one of whether to one of when, where, and how. Within days of the decision, a host of German politicians were debating potential criteria, the utility of the experience of key allies (e.g., PDD-25), the CNN factor, how to decide when to say yes or no, and how to avoid being drawn into conflicts where Germany has no interests, etc.

On July 14, 1994—i.e., the day of the German Supreme Court ruling—the German Defense Minister also issued planning guidance for the future development of the Bundeswehr entitled "Conceptional Guidance for the Future Development of the Bundeswehr."[1] These guidelines represent the fruition of some two years of internal deliberations on how to restructure the Bundeswehr for non–Article 5 missions. On March 15, 1995, the German Cabinet gave its stamp of approval to an updated and more detailed set of plans finalizing the Bundeswehr's new structure, the plans for the individual services, the units earmarked for specific missions, as well as base closures.[2] Taken together, these two documents provide a de facto blueprint of

---

[1]See *Konzeptionelle Leitlinie zur Weiterentwicklung der Bundeswehr* (Bonn: Bundesminister der Verteidigung, July 12, 1994).

[2]See *Ressortkonzept zur Anpassung der Streitkräftestrukturen, der Territorialen Wehrverwaltung und der Stationierung* (Bonn: Bundesminister der Verteidigung, March 15, 1995).

German plans to build military capabilities from which a future German contribution to peacekeeping will be drawn.

It remains to be seen how well this blueprint holds up in German politics and under the pressure of real world events.   The Bundeswehr has nevertheless crossed a political and conceptual Rubicon. Built and trained as part of NATO's original military mission of deterring and, if necessary, defending West Germany as a front-line state against a Soviet-led Warsaw Pact invasion, the Bundeswehr has had its rationale, mission, size, and structure overhauled. Perhaps no institution in German society has undergone as radical a transformation as the German Bundeswehr since the end of the Cold War.

While this process was initiated under former Defense Minister Gerhard Stoltenberg in the period immediately following the collapse of communism, the new plans have the handwriting of Volker Rühe. Rühe has put the Bundeswehr at the cutting edge of the unification process, often referring to the integrating role of the Bundeswehr as one of the key motors in the unification process. The Bundeswehr has undergone a three-phase process of restructuring. The first phase was the integration of the German armed forces following unification. This was followed by a second phase devoted to the standardization and de facto West Germanization of the Bundeswehr in the new eastern states. The final phase has been the reorientation of the Bundeswehr toward a new and broader set of missions.

Rühe's new planning guidelines, issued on July 12, 1994 along with the Cabinet decision of mid-March 1995, constitute the overall framework and plans for this third phase. The German Bundeswehr will be reduced from 370,000 to 340,000 by 1996. This will include some 290,000 Main Defense Forces (MDF) and some 50,000 Crisis Reaction Forces (CRF).[3] While the main task of the Bundeswehr remains the protection of Germany, the new guidelines lay out an officially sanctioned new risk assessment and political requirements, emphasizing that German forces must also be available for peacekeeping missions and crisis management missions.

---

[3]The precise breakdowns for the CRF are 37,000 for the army; 12,300 for the air force; and 4,300 for the navy.

As a result of these new tasks, the emphasis is on the mobility, flexibility and multifunctionality of German forces. German forces are no longer structured for one specific operational scenario, but for a spectrum of scenarios. The MDF will no longer be tailored for a largely static concept of forward defense as during the Cold War, but will instead be reoriented toward flexible counter-concentration. This will require a greater emphasis on joint operations, enhanced mobility, and more flexible force postures. At the same time, the greater warning time for any threat means that readiness standards for these forces can be relaxed in the existing strategic environment.

The new CRF, on the other hand, are designed to consist of combat-ready rapidly available forces for operations in either a NATO, WEU, or UN framework under any and all geographical and climatic conditions.

The overall number of German divisions will be reduced from 8 to 7. The overall number of brigades will be reduced to 22. They will consist of 6 combat-ready CRF brigades; 4 combat-ready MDF brigades which can complement or relieve the CRF brigades; 4 substantially ready MDF brigades each with 3 combat-ready battalions from which 4 further brigades could be formed; and 8 partially mobilized MDF brigades each with 2 battalions of combat-ready forces from which 2 further battalions could be formed.

Senior German military leaders emphasize that Germany's Main Reaction Forces continue to constitute the backbone of Germany's contribution to NATO and the balance of power in the heart of Europe. The Bundeswehr's primary function remains what it has been in the past, namely, the backbone of defense in Central Europe. However, the creation of the new CRF is the main new development and the one we will focus on, for it is from these capabilities that the German peacekeeping capabilities will flow. Building the CRF is also the Bundeswehr's top priority. Spending for and the modernization of the MDF will essentially be frozen until late in this decade to focus on the creation of the CRF.[4]

---

[4]In late August 1994, in a confidential meeting with senior military leaders, Chancellor Kohl pledged that the German defense budget would be increased slightly to DM 47.9 billion (up from DM 47.5 billion) and would then remain constant measured in real terms until 1998 when it would be increased to DM 48.4 billion. Further savings are

The Crisis Reaction Forces have three missions. They are designed, first, to contribute to territorial defense. Second, they are also available for in-region defense throughout the territory of the Atlantic Alliance, as well as to contribute to NATO's or the WEU's future crisis management capabilities. They, therefore, will include the German contribution to NATO's AMF (L), the Eurocorps, the ARRC, the MND (C), and to the NATO Composite Force (NCF). Third and finally, it is from these assets that the future German peacekeeping contribution under either the UN or the OSCE will be drawn. As Klaus Naumann has put it, the purpose of the CRF is to allow Germany to participate in both peacekeeping and crisis management missions to prevent and contain conflicts to keep wars away from German soil.

The Crisis Reaction Forces will include:

- Six light, mechanized, air-mobile and air-mechanized brigades with their combat support and logistics components.

- Six air force squadrons for attack, air defense, and reconnaissance missions, two mixed SAM wings, and three mixed air transport wings as well as helicopters for search and rescue missions.

- Two naval task forces of two to three frigates each with the corresponding mine warfare and naval air arm assets. The German navy will also have the capability to transport a small peacekeeping contingent—about one army battalion—and to serve as command headquarters for that unit.

In mid-March, Bonn officially announced the earmarking of key units in both the Main and Crisis Reaction Forces. The Reaction Forces brigades will consist of the 31st airborne brigade in Oldenburg

---

also expected from the decision to shorten the length of conscription from 12 to 10 months and the planned reduction of the overall size of the Bundeswehr to 340,000 by 1996. These savings will be channeled into modernization plans for the new CRF. See *Die Welt am Sonntag*, August 28, 1994. These budgetary figures were subsequently confirmed in the new coalition agreement of the German government after the fall 1994 national elections. They were presented as the financial foundation for future Bundeswehr planning to the parliament on March 15, 1995. According to Bundeswehr Inspector General Klaus Naumann, these measures will allow for a 30 percent capital investment slice in the defense budget. See Naumann, op. cit., p. 13.

and the 37th mechanized infantry brigade in Frankenburg, which will become a light mobile brigade; the 21st infantry brigade in Augustdorf and the 12th infantry brigade in Amberg, which will become a mechanized infantry brigade; and an air-mechanized brigade in Fritzleben as well as the German component of the Franco-German brigade in Müllheim.

Main Defense Forces and Crisis Reaction Forces will also be combined at brigade level. Crisis Reaction Force battalions will, for example, be subordinated to Main Defense Force brigades. Similarly, Main Defense Force battalions will be subordinated to Crisis Reaction Force brigades. Thus, even in the air-mechanized brigade MDF elements will be present in the CRF battalions. Accordingly, CRF elements will also be prominent in the Main Defense Forces: the 26th airborne brigade in Saarlouis; the 39th mechanized infantry brigade in Erfurt; the 40th mechanized infantry brigade in Schwerin; and the 23rd mountain brigade in Bad Reichenhall. Finally, the 25th brigade command in Calw will be transformed into a Special Forces command. By establishing this command, the armed forces will have forces for emergency sorties such as the evacuation of German citizens. The 25th paratrooper battalion in Calw, the long-range scouting companies of the corps, and commando companies of the airborne brigades will be combined under this command.

In the air force, the CRF elements will consist of the 71st fighter squadron in Wittmund and the 74th fighter squadron in Neuburg an der Donau, the 51st reconnaissance squadron in Jagel as well as the 31st fighter bomber squadron in Nörvenich, the 32nd fighter bomber squadron in Lechfeld, and the 34th fighter bomber squadron in Memmingen. They will also include the 1st air defense SAM squadron in Heide and the 3rd air defense SAM squadron in Oldenburg. Finally, they will also include three air transport squadrons: the 61st in Penzing, the 62nd in Wunstdorf, and the 63rd in Mohn.

The Crisis Reaction Forces are designed to simultaneously allow for one major operation (i.e., up to an army division along with corresponding air assets) and simultaneous participation in smaller missions—i.e., peacekeeping, humanitarian assistance, and evacuations.[5] These forces will be designed to meet NATO readiness standards—i.e., small numbers will be ready to deploy within 48 hours, others in 3–7 days, and the entire contingent within 15–30 days. Because of these higher standards (and because of the political sensitivities associated with a conscript army engaged in missions beyond territorial defense), 80–85 percent will consist of professional soldiers. The remaining conscripts will consist of volunteers. The maximal duration of a mission is foreseen as six months. How long will it take for the Bundeswehr to implement these ambitious plans? German MoD officials state that two battalions will be ready for peacekeeping by the end of 1994 with one full brigade available in 1995. All Crisis Reaction Forces are scheduled to be operational by 1998/1989.[6]

A number of important questions concerning the Bundeswehr's future have not been fully resolved. The following examples are illustrative of the issues German military leaders will continue to wrestle with. The first is whether and how Bonn will be able to avoid the de facto creation of a two-tiered Bundeswehr, with the Crisis Reaction Forces becoming the top priority both in terms of funds and highly qualified personnel. Senior German leaders strenuously deny that this is their intent. They point to the steps they have taken to insure this does not happen. To guard against this danger, the Bundeswehr's new structure deliberately enmeshes Crisis Reaction and Main Defense Force units. German military leaders insist that it is perfectly normal for the Bundeswehr to have a division of labor when it comes to missions, and that they are planning to maintain organic ties between the Main Defense and Crisis Reaction Forces so that units can rotate in and out of each over time. How successfully this works out remains to be seen.[7]

---

[5]In the words of the Bundeswehr's Inspector General Klaus Naumann: "We can assume that larger-scale operations involving combat will be conducted in only one conflict area at any one time. It will therefore suffice to maintain a contingent with the size of a present-day army division, plus the relevant air force and navy elements . . . . For rotation and reinforcement purposes we will maintain a second contingent of approximately the same size. This will give Germany sufficient possibilities to participate in NATO, WEU, and UN operations." Ibid., p. 13.

[6]See Günther Gillessen, "Erleichterung in der Bundeswehr," *Frankfurter Allgemeine Zeitung*, July 29, 1994.

[7]See, for example, Franz Mendel, "Eine Zwei-Klassen Armee," *Europäische Sicherheit*, No. 6, 1994, p. 267. See the interview with Army Chief of Staff Lieutenant General

Second, future training is also central to how the Bundeswehr prepares itself for these missions. In late August 1994, the Chief of Staff of the German Army, Hartmut Bagger, issued new policy guidance for the training of German army units for future peace support operations. Following the principle of the multifunctionality of forces, the guidance emphasized that training for peace support missions should be seen as a complement to standard training, not as a substitute. Again, it remains to be seen how the Bundeswehr strikes the appropriate balance in meeting the training needs for a Crisis Reaction Force that on paper is expected to meet widely divergent operational needs ranging from consensual peacekeeping to combat operations. Whether the intense but short training periods currently envisioned are sufficient to prepare units for such diverse future missions remains to be seen.

In addition to earmarking units for certain types of missions, the Bundeswehr has established a special school in Hammelburg for UN peace support operations. In addition to familiarizing officers and NCOs with UN peace support procedures, this school will provide specialized training in a variety of areas—staff officers for UN missions, military observers, logistics specialists, military policemen and combat engineers. It will offer special intensive courses (usually three weeks in duration) for units preparing to deploy in peace support missions. The courses will be taught in English and will include non-German participants. German officers will also be trained at the UN Logistic Officer Course (UNLOC) in Norway as well as the UN Military Police Course (UNMILPOC) in Denmark.

A third example of a key issue the Bundeswehr needs to resolve concerns future command structures. Senior MoD officials have singled out this issue, along with logistics and training, as the key areas that the Bundeswehr must make its top priorities. The end of the Cold War and the growing involvement of the German armed forces in non–Article 5 missions have forced Bonn to think about the creation of a national command structure. Although initial German involvement in peacekeeping operations was handled on a task-force basis, the experience the Bundeswehr gathered in Cambodia and Somalia convinced the senior MoD leadership of the need for improved na-

---

Hartmut Bagger, "Die Idee einer Zwei-Klassen Armee ist falsch," *Frankfurter Rundschau* July 28, 1994.

tional command structures in peacetime to be better able to prepare for such contingencies as well as to command German forces engaged in such non–Article 5 operations.

Already following the Gulf War, German defense experts pointed to the need for new national command structures for operations outside the traditional NATO command structure. Uwe Nerlich, for example, argued that Germany had to partially renationalize its own command structures to become a normal European strategic actor like its allies if it was to become capable of participating in future multilateral coalitions acting in non–Article 5 scenarios. According to Nerlich:

> A certain renationalization of not only our analysis, but also the decisionmaking structure, is simply structurally necessary under the conditions that are emerging for the 1990s. This results from the changed nature of the threat, and especially from the very different crisis dynamic that is emerging and which underlies the new American global strategy. The dynamics of future crises will be radically different than they have been in the past. This means that in the early phase of a crisis, a country like the Federal Republic will have to make national decisions. Whether the Federal Republic wants to or not, it will not have in Europe the type of multinational context in which such decisions can be made pending the achievement of a Political Union. This underscores the fact that the structures and regulations of the NATO system will increasingly lead to a strengthened renationalization according to the type of consultations envisioned in Article 4 of the Washington Treaty. . . . There must be a reexamination of the problems and necessity of national decisions about the use of multilateral instruments. The previous German policy, a policy of total integration in multilateral structures, will, if not always, eventually reach its limits.[8]

In the spring of 1991, Major General Klaus Reinhardt, Commandant of the Bundeswehr Command College in Hamburg, underscored the need for the creation of a small German national staff to complement the German planning conducted within the NATO structure for possible German participation in either UN-led or NATO operations

---

[8]See Uwe Nerlich, "Deutsche Sicherheitspolitik und Konflikte ausserhalb des NATO-Gebiets," *Europa Archiv*, No. 10, 1991, pp. 303–310.

conducted outside of the Article 5 context.   In the words of Reinhardt:

> The tradition of an exclusive General Staff with its own career path has not been adopted in the Bundeswehr. A restoration of the General Staff as an autonomous high-level military authority outside of the ministry in the way that existed at the time of von Moltke is no longer appropriate for many reasons. Today, many of the tasks which previously were undertaken in the General Staff have been divided among many positions both within and outside of the ministry. For professional as well as political reasons the decisive competence for the command of troops was transferred to NATO at the time of the founding of the Bundeswehr.
>
> Nevertheless, the previous regulation of the spectrum of tasks for the Bundeswehr is no longer adequate in light of the radically changed security policy situation of Germany that has emerged after unification and the Gulf War. A national staff for limited national planning and implementation, for example in the context of the United Nations, will be required. Such a staff can only be envisioned as a complement to and not a substitute for the proven integrated structures of NATO authorities. We have initiated thoughts in this direction.[9]

Given the historical baggage of a "German General Staff," this has been a red-button issue in the German media and on the German political scene. Post-war Germany deliberately set up a military structure without a General Staff headed by a strong institutional figure. The powers of the Inspector General of the Bundeswehr remain quite limited. Attempts to update these arrangements for the new challenges facing the Bundeswehr have been viewed by many with suspicion. There have been several articles, for example, attacking the current Inspector General, General Klaus Naumann, who has been the point man in thinking about how to reform German command structures, accusing him of wanting to recreate the German

---

[9]See the speech by Major General Klaus Reinhardt, Commandant of the Bundeswehr Command College in Hamburg, entitled "Gedanken zur Persönlichkeit, Amt und Wirken des Generalfeldmarschalls Helmut Graf von Moltke aus heutiger Sicht," delivered before the Moltke-Stiftung in Berlin upon the occasion of the commemoration of the 100th anniversary of the death of Field Marshall Helmut Graf von Moltke on April 24, 1991.

General Staff.[10] On July 22, 1994, the German Defense Ministry issued new planning guidance drawn up by Naumann calling for the creation of a new national command structure in the context of the new Crisis Reaction Forces. These guidelines called for the development of plans for flexible structures capable of national peacetime operational control for the purpose of training and exercises; peace support operations outside of Germany and outside of NATO structures; and crisis management and combat operations outside of Germany but conducted under NATO auspices.

In January 1995, Bonn created a joint service command and control center—called the Führungszentrum—for future peacekeeping missions. Established provisionally for a one-year period, it has been added as a new staff division to the existing armed forces command structure. Its responsibilities will include operational planning as well as the operational command of future peacekeeping missions. It will be responsible for coordinating the missions of relatively small units from the three services. It integrates previous ad hoc arrangements, such as that set up for the Somali missions. Its future status will be reviewed after an initial one-year trial period. A forthcoming decree will clarify whether it will have overall control of peacekeeping units or whether the command will have to be channeled through the respective services.[11]

A fourth question is how Bonn plans to finance future peacekeeping operations. Since 1990, the German defense budget has been reduced nearly 25 percent in real terms. Future peacekeeping missions will come at a time when there is already serious debate and controversy over both a two-tiered as well as a "hollow" Bundeswehr. The SPD, for example, not only continues to oppose German participation in combat missions beyond NATO borders, but has proposed a further reduction of the Bundeswehr to a level of 300,000, claiming that the planned level of 340,000 will not be sustainable in light of budget difficulties.[12] Moreover, how does one find the right balance

---

[10]See, for example, Wolfgang Hoffmann, "Ein Generalstab?" *Die Zeit*, No. 33, August 12, 1994.

[11]See Karl Feldmeyer, "Bundeswehr erhält Führungszentrum," *Frankfurter Allgemeine Zeitung*, January 3, 1995.

[12]See, for example, the interview with SPD defense spokesperson Walter Kolbow, *dpa*, October 14, 1994.

not only between Main Defense and Crisis Reaction Forces? From where does one draw the funds for unanticipated peacekeeping missions? In 1992, for example, the overseas mission of the Bundeswehr cost an estimated DM 78 million.[13] In 1993, these costs rose to some DM 418 million,[14] and about DM 180 million was set aside for 1994. In 1992, such missions were DM 224 million over budget, causing additional strain on an already stretched defense budget.

The SPD opposition has called for the creation of a special operating budget for peacekeeping operations. In this manner, according to Karsten Voigt, foreign policy spokesman of the SPD, both the government and the parliament would be forced to clarify German priorities, objectives, as well as limits. Thus far, the government has rejected such notions, insisting that it is impossible in practical terms to plan for such missions because one can hardly anticipate crises.

A fifth example of the kind of questions that still need to be resolved regarding the future of the Bundeswehr concerns roles and missions. The Bundeswehr's efforts to retool itself for a new set of missions under the mantles of crisis management and peacekeeping have rekindled old arguments over the proper distribution of roles and missions among the German armed services. Although the army has dominated German military thinking historically, as well as that of the Bundeswehr in the post-war period, some strategists have argued that the role of the German air and naval forces should now be upgraded as they are better equipped for many of these new potential missions.

According to this argument, German air and naval forces require little if any restructuring and are, therefore, essentially ready to participate in these new missions today. Moreover, the greater mobility and projection capabilities of these services may make them better suited for many new missions the Bundeswehr might face. Finally, it

---

[13]The cost breakdown for 1992 ran as follows: DM 34 million for air transport for the UN in Iraq; DM 12 million for the Adriatic embargo; DM 11 million each for Somalia and Cambodia; and DM 8 million for air transport in Bosnia-Hercegovina.

[14]In 1993, operations in Somalia cost about DM 264 million; DM 65 million for the Adriatic embargo; DM 34 million for air transport in Bosnia-Hercegovina; DM 20 million each for Cambodia and Iraq; and DM 16 million in transport costs for allied forces in the former Yugoslavia. For further details see "Wieviel kosten Auslandseinsätze der Bundeswehr?" *Frankfurter Allgmeine Zeitung,* July 30, 1994.

is argued that the fact that these services rely less on conscripts may make their use less controversial back home.

Senior German army leaders have strenuously objected, claiming that the army must remain the backbone of a continental power such as Germany, that it is the glue that holds Germany's alliances together, and that ground forces remain essential for future peacekeeping operations as well. They insist that the current fascination with light forces is misleading and point to the American, French, and British experiences with peace support operations. In the words of retired German Army General Hans Henning von Sandrat, former NATO Commander-in-Chief Central Europe, the army's role will be essential for the future success of the Bundeswehr in peace support operations:

> Although the restructuring of the army for the new spectrum of missions will lead to a shift in priorities from heavy ground forces to light forces, above all air mobile or air mechanized forces, the current widespread impression that Crisis Reaction Forces can consist only of light forces is erroneous. The Crisis Reaction Forces must consist of a balanced mixture of heavy mechanized, light and air mobile troops, including armored helicopters in order to have the necessary resilience, penetrability, active and passive defense capabilities, and the technological superiority that will be required even in limited missions—not only because the Crisis Reaction Forces are the first wave of alliance and territorial defense, but also because peace support operations, including the defense of humanitarian missions, also require heavy elements. England uses heavy mechanized tank battalions for humanitarian assistance![15]

Such questions notwithstanding, senior German military officials insist that Germany has made enormous progress in a relatively short period of time, especially in terms of the attitudes of the armed forces themselves. In a recent speech in Washington, General Klaus Naumann pointed to this change in mentality as one of the most important changes that has taken place in terms of preparing the Bundeswehr for future peacekeeping operations. In his words:

---

[15]See the article by retired Army General and former AFCENT Commander Hans Henning von Sandrat, "Künftige Rolle und Aufgabe des Heers," Europäische Sicherheit, No. 6, 1994, pp. 276–286.

I am pleased to report that the attitude of German officers and NCOs has changed considerably in the last two years. Some of you will recall that during the Gulf War there were individual members of the German air force who took their apprehensions about operating out of Turkey public. That kind of faintheartedness has vanished. I had occasion to be on board one of our nightly relief flights to Bosnia and Hercegovina and was shocked by the extent of anti-aircraft activity from the ground. But the plane's crew reacted very calmly, with the pilot coolly saying: "Well, General, we are going to take her up a bit to the left now. They are doing this every night, as we found out, but they never manage to hit us." There was not a trace of nervousness or a sense that something special was happening. Rather, everything was handled as a matter of routine. This I interpret as a positive change which leads me to believe that a few years hence we will have a capable force, ready to go, and willing to participate in international operations alongside our partners.[16]

Questions about how to prepare the Bundeswehr militarily for future peacekeeping missions have been matched by a new political debate over what criteria should be applied in deciding where Germany should contribute its armed forces as well as how and who should make those decisions. In the immediate aftermath of the German Supreme Court's ruling, Chancellor Kohl and others made a point of stating that "Germans to the front" was not Bonn's policy. Along with Foreign Minister Kinkel and Defense Minister Rühe, all senior Bonn officials emphasized that the Federal Republic would continue to emphasize crisis prevention and nonmilitary means for crisis resolution.

At the same time, German officials and parliamentarians have openly debated the criteria that should be used for deciding when to say yes or no to a request for German forces for a peacekeeping operation. After an initial attempt to examine the experience of many of its key allies in attempting to define criteria, German officials backed off from listing specific criteria. They have instead opted for establishing a set of general principles and treating each possible deployment case by case. The concern has been that criteria could easily lead to a

---

[16]See General Klaus Naumann, "Euro-American Security Challenges—Germany's Role and Responsibility," *Transatlantic Brief #9*, Konrad Adenauer Stiftung, July 1994, pp. 5–6.

kind of automaticity, thereby limiting Bonn's diplomatic leeway. The principles thus far articulated in public and private by leading officials in both the foreign and defense ministries include:

1. Germany has no automatic obligation to the UN or OSCE. Bonn retains the right to refuse requests and to decide its involvement case by case.

2. Germany's future military role will be determined by values and German national interests as well as its alliance obligations. The existence of a clear international mandate is an important precondition for Bundeswehr participation.

3. Germany's priority will be peacekeeping missions in and around Europe. Multilateral involvement, especially of Bonn's allies in NATO and the WEU, will be critical. The greater the participation of Bonn's allies, the more likely German participation will be. However, the involvement of Germany's key allies should not be viewed as creating any kind of automaticity for German involvement.

4. History should not determine where German troops can go—i.e., German troops can go where the Wehrmacht has been, *provided* that their presence is viewed as a stabilizing factor. In some cases past German history may be a reason to get involved, in others it may be a reason to stay out. The consent of the parties involved in the conflict will be an important factor.

5. The principle of subsidiarity—i.e., regional organizations and powers—should be in the forefront of resolving regional crises.

6. There must be a credible political prospect for the success of the mission. The greater the dangers the more crucial it is that there be a clear timetable and concept for political success. For combat operations, the danger to German interests must be clear and there must be a broad consensus in parliament as well as in public opinion.

7. There must be a requirement for a political mandate through the OSCE or the UN as well as an achievable set of operational goals. Following the Somalian experience, German officials emphasized that it may be better not to get involved in an operation than to have to withdraw in failure.

What these criteria mean in practice, however, has already proven to be a point of some tension. German officials admit that they realize how high the pent-up demand is for peacekeeping contributions, but they are concerned that they will be sucked into any number of operations where German interests are not clear and the prospects of success not high. The German press has already reported about alleged tensions between Foreign Minster Kinkel and Defense Minister Rühe over where the Bundeswehr might be deployed. Kinkel, a strong proponent of expanding German support for the UN, has been sympathetic to requests from UN Secretary General Boutros-Boutros Ghali for contributing German troops to future UN peacekeeping missions.

Rühe, having played a key role in liberating the German armed forces from the legal and political constraints of the Cold War era, has been much more reserved. Whereas the UN always plays a prominent role in Kinkel's policy pronouncement, Rühe is much more reserved, for example, preferring to emphasize the Bundeswehr's need to plan future missions with its close allies in NATO. Rühe has argued, for example, that NATO has much more credibility in the eyes of the German public than the UN. He has often warned about Germany getting involved in peacekeeping operations in far-flung places where the German interest was not obvious, pointing to the U.S. experience in Somalia. He has often pointed to the problems of UNPROFOR in the former Yugoslavia and voiced his concern about the Bundeswehr getting involved in an operation where the mission was not well thought through or the forces were not adequate for carrying it out. If German forces are to be involved, he has argued, the conditions must be the right ones lest a budding German consensus in favor of peacekeeping and a new role for the Bundeswehr be shattered.[17]

The SPD opposition has also tabled its own list of criteria, criticizing the ruling coalition for being too focused on narrow "German interests." In the words of the SPD's foreign policy spokesman Karsten Voigt, Bonn must also take broader European interests into account

---

[17]See, for example, Rühe's interview on Bundeswehr participation in peacekeeping operations in *Die Welt*, November 27, 1994; his interview "Wir drängeln uns nicht vor," *Der Spiegel*, No. 2, January 9, 1995; as well as the article "Kinkel und Rühe streiten über UNO-Engagement, *Die Welt*, January 23, 1995.

as well as the viability of multilateral institutions such as the UN which German foreign policy wants to strengthen.[18] At the same time, the SPD clearly remains divided over the degree to which it should or should not support Bundeswehr participation in such missions. While the SPD leadership led by Rudolf Sharping have pushed the party to accept the letter and the spirit of the Constitutional Court ruling on the Bundeswehr, rank-and-file sentiment against growing Bundeswehr involvement remains strong, especially in the party's left wing for whom a limited German military role was a source of pride.

However, the debate over Bundeswehr participation in a possible withdrawal of UNPROFOR from the former Yugoslavia showed just how divided the party remains. Whereas Sharping initially signaled his support for the Alliance request for German Tornados, for example, figures such as Oskar LaFontaine immediately criticized him as being too accommodating to the CDU-led coalition and abandoning past SPD policy supporting only traditional consensual peacekeeping missions.[19] While the Tornado issue showed just how divided the SPD remains on many core foreign and security policy issues, this was hardly comforting news for the CDU-led coalition. Not only does it enjoy a very narrow majority in the Bundestag, but the Kohl government has underscored its desire to have the broadest political and public support possible for Bundeswehr deployments beyond NATO's borders.[20]

For obvious reasons, the first several test cases will be important for solidifying the emerging German consensus over peacekeeping. Ideally, Bonn is looking for a case where German interests are clearly

---

[18]According to Voigt: "The Americans see this question in terms of 'What are our national interests?' We Germans must ask ourselves not only what is at stake for German foreign policy, but what is at stake for the European Union and the international community. To reduce it to the narrow question of what is in our national interests is not enough." As quoted in *Deutscher Bundestag, Stenographischer Bericht*, op. cit.

[19]See, for example, the speech by SPD Party Chairman Rudolf Sharping at the February 1995 Wehrkunde conference, author's private copy. In contrast, see the interview with Oskar LaFontaine, "Keine Tornados nach Bosnien," *Die Zeit*, No. 12, March 17, 1995.

[20]For further details on the intra-SPD debate, see Günter Bannas, "In der SPD wächst das Missbehagen über aussenpolitische Orientierungslosigkeit der Partei," *Frankfurter Allgemeine Zeitung*, January 17, 1995.

engaged, where all of its allies are engaged, and where the prospects for success are high. No one wants the initial German experience to fail, thereby running the risk of a major political and psychological setback. The real world may not be so kind. The dilemma for Germany is that German interests are often most directly engaged in regions or conflicts where the prospects for success may not be clear. Bosnia is the obvious case where important German interests are at stake, yet the shadow of history and the poor prospects for clear-cut success have made Bonn cautious. As Foreign Minister Klaus Kinkel wrote recently:

> Our history has imposed on us a special moral responsibility for preserving peace. At the same time, however, it explains why Germans must observe particular restraint in using military force. This year is the fiftieth anniversary of the decisive events which led to Germany's defeat in a war unleashed by Germany itself. The memories of this time remain equally vivid in the minds of those who made great sacrifices for the victory of freedom and of those who were forced to serve as the helpless tools of the Nazi war machine. For 10 years after the war, the Federal Republic of Germany had no armed forces of its own. For half a century no German soldier has taken part in life-and-death acts of war.

> Even now that the question of constitutional admissibility has been answered, the issue of when and to what end German soldiers are to be deployed in situations other than national and NATO defense remains highly explosive. No matter where such a mission takes place, it will set a precedent with far-reaching implications. It must be firmly accepted at home and abroad. It would not be in the interest of Germany or Europe, nor would it benefit peace, if future German participation in armed missions were to undermine the trust in Germany's peaceful nature which, since 1945, has become the basis of an ever closer relationship between democratic Germany and the former enemies of the Hitler regime.[21]

Last, but by no means least, Germany must also sort out the modalities on how to decide on the use of German armed forces, including peacekeeping operations. While the German Constitutional Court

---

[21]See Klaus Kinkel, "Peacekeeping Missions: Germany Can Now Play Its Part," *NATO Review*, No. 5, October 1994, p. 5.

decreed that only a simple majority in the Bundestag is required for the use of German armed forces, the wrestling match over the proper balance between executive and legislative authority has already begun between the government and the Bundestag. While the German party system certainly guarantees that a chancellor has much more leverage over his party in the Bundestag than, for example, a U.S. president has over Congress, it is also clear that the key committees in the Bundestag plan to play an important role. The German government has also underscored its interest in establishing as broad a base of political support as possible for future Bundeswehr operations, including the parliamentary opposition. The latter may be a necessity given the narrow majority the CDU-led government currently enjoys in the Bundestag. But it also reflects the desire by German political leaders to prevent Bundeswehr missions from becoming partisan and polarizing issues in German politics.

Chapter Five

UNANSWERED QUESTIONS

Germany has taken important steps in terms of clarifying the political and legal foundation for a future peacekeeping role. Moreover, the German Ministry of Defense has over the past three years launched an ambitious attempt to restructure the Bundeswehr for a new set of missions. The clear priority in this restructuring process has been to prepare the Bundeswehr for future crisis management and peacekeeping missions. These priorities are reflected both in the plans for the creation of the German Crisis Reaction Forces and in German modernization plans. In principle and on paper, the Bundeswehr is on its way toward creating substantial new capabilities that future peacekeeping missions could draw on.

Most important, the terms of the debate have changed. It is no longer a question of whether Germany will participate in non–Article 5 missions, but where, when, and how. In this context, the German debate has unfolded in ways not that dissimilar from our own. Despite the call for clear criteria for future decisionmaking, the government quickly discovered that the downside of establishing such criteria was that they could constrain future governmental decisionmaking and lead to a kind of undesired automaticity. Although some German politicians initially called for Bonn to draw up the German equivalent of PDD-25, thus far the result of the German government's own internal policy review has been a very general set of principles and criteria clearly designed to give the German government flexibility to decide case by case when to say yes or no.

A number of key questions remain unanswered. The first and, in many ways, most important issue is how Germans will define their interests and where will they see them as sufficiently engaged to justify German participation in future peacekeeping missions. The easy answer one hears in Bonn is "in and around Europe." German involvement in Cambodia, Iraq, and Somalia was crucial in terms of setting political precedents, gathering hands-on experience, and supporting institutions and allies upon which German security depends, be they NATO or the UN. However, Germany's priority remains dealing with potential instability that could directly affect Germany or its neighbors.

If ones digs a bit deeper, one also discovers an undertone in the German debate, most openly articulated by the SPD-led opposition but latent across the political spectrum, that Germany should not allow itself to be "dragged into" conflicts by other powers or even close allies pursuing their own national agendas. Specifically, German SPD politicians have warned against being dragged into the "former colonial conflicts" of countries such as France or the United Kingdom. One also hears voices expressing similar concern about U.S.-led military adventurism.

Instead, Social Democratic leaders have called for a much broader calculus to determine when and where German armed forces should be used, one tied less to narrow national interests and more to Germany's broader responsibilities and commitment to multilateralism and institutions such as the UN. This still reflects the idealistic and moral streak in the German peacekeeping debate, which assumes that involvement in peace operations where there are no enemies, just belligerents requiring varying degrees of coercion or reassurance to get them to stop fighting, is both morally superior and politically easier than, for example, Bundeswehr involvement in a coalition of the willing in a Persian Gulf War.

It remains to be seen how well such views fare when the human and material costs of peacekeeping, as well as the thorny issue of domestic political support and sustainability, become evident. Looking back at the experience of the Clinton administration over the past two years, one wonders whether German politicians will really be any more willing to risk German treasure and lives for the principles of multilateralism or the United Nations than Americans were.[1] One of the ironies in the current situation is that Germany is turning toward multilateral peacekeeping at a time when the United States may be turning against it, and that Germany's interest in defending human rights and upholding international law may cross with a declining American interest to do so. Time will tell whether German politicians will be able to more effectively tie their definitions of German vital interests to such objectives and defend them in public than American politicians have been able to do on their own home front.

A second crucial and as yet unanswered question is how well the Bundeswehr will perform in future peace support operations. Bonn has now resolved the legal issues that had heretofore constrained Germany from assuming such a role. The German Ministry of Defense has designed an impressive plan that on paper will create significant peacekeeping capabilities. Yet, these same forces are in theory supposed to be able to handle the full range of missions beyond territorial defense. It is one thing to let a handful of air crews brave relatively ineffective ground fire en route to a humanitarian airlift in Sarajevo in an activity sanctioned by both the UN and NATO. It is quite another to put a brigade of German infantry in the path of a resolute and well-armed enemy hundreds of kilometers from Germany's borders as part of a coalition of the willing. There are important qualitative differences which, in turn, pose very different demands in terms of preparing German forces for the future. Unfortunately, many of the future crisis management and crisis response missions that one can envision "in and around Europe" may be more like the latter than the former. Although the Bundeswehr was widely seen as a very effective fighting force during the Cold War, time will tell how fragile or cohesive German forces will prove to be when asked to operate outside the Alliance or in a completely new and foreign environment.

That, of course, requires that these troops be as well prepared as possible militarily for the demands and missions they may face in the future. The crux of the practical military problem for the Bundes-

---

[1] On the American experience, see Ronald D. Asmus, "The Rise and Fall of Multilateralism: America's New Foreign Policy and What It Means for Europe," in Marco Carnovale (ed.), *European Security and International Institutions After the Cold War* (London: Macmillan Press, Ltd. 1995).

wehr lies in the structure of the German military and can be summed up in one sentence: How can the German military be made capable of power projection operations without raising fears that it is taking on a new, offensive-minded orientation? Yet it is precisely those capabilities that may be the key to success in future missions. Bonn has deliberately created a rather modest and all-purpose crisis management capability designed to operate with its allies in a future team effort to not arouse the suspicions of its neighbors. However, given the general state of high-technology weapons, the size of foreign arsenals, and similar concerns, is even a single division's worth of power projection capability enough for a country with the interests that Germany has?

Third, Germany is starting to experience the kinds of debates that will sound all too familiar to an American audience. How does one decide criteria for future missions in practice? How involved should civilians become in detailed military operational planning? What is the proper balance between executive and legislative authority in decisionmaking processes? No doubt the German debate will also soon experience controversies over the relative merits of limited vs. decisive force. On all these issues, Germans will approach them through their own optic, one that is shaped by their own history and experience. Germany is at the beginning of a new learning curve, forced to deal with an entire set of issues it was spared from facing in the past because of the limited mandate of the Bundeswehr.

Fourth, the evolution of German public opinion on this issue will be crucial. A series of public opinion polls commissioned by RAND since the fall of the Berlin Wall on German public attitudes on nationals security issues, for example, has shown just how German public sentiments are shifting in the post–Cold War era. Germans are starting to define a new set of national interests beyond their border. They support the notion of a unified Germany assuming more responsibility, including in the realm of security policy. By overwhelming margins they support the principle of German participation in peacekeeping operations. Moreover, they are not pacifists but often support the use of force in principle to defend human rights or to uphold international law.

The sticking point has always been whether and how Germans *themselves* should participate in such efforts. For these polls also show that Germany's "culture of reticence" is a major factor. The German public remains skittish about the use of the Bundeswehr in combat missions. Support on this front remains low, although it has started to inch up. It is also strongest among German youth, especially in western Germany, who wish Germany to assume the same responsibilities as its neighbors and allies.[2] Political leadership will be essential to insure that this shift continues.

Germany has come a long way since the collapse of communism in redefining its foreign policy interests and role and determining how a new Bundeswehr fits into that broader vision. The crux of the practical political problem for Bonn is that when it does decide to employ the Bundeswehr in peace support operations, the rationale and German interest must be clear, its key allies must be involved under a clear mandate, and such missions must be a success lest the emerging new consensus in favor of a German military role be shattered.

---

[2]See Ronald D. Asmus, *German Strategy and Opinion After the Wall 1990–1993* (Santa Monica, Calif.: RAND, MR-444-FNF/OSD/A/AF, 1994).

BIBLIOGRAPHY

Asmus, Ronald D., *German Strategy and Opinion After the Wall 1990–1993* (Santa Monica, Calif.: RAND, MR-444-FNF/OSD/A/AF, 1994).

Asmus, Ronald D., *Germany After the Gulf War* (Santa Monica, Calif.: RAND, N-3391-AF, 1992).

Asmus, Ronald D., *German Unification and Its Ramifications* (Santa Monica, Calif.: RAND, R-4021-A, 1991).

Kinkel, Klaus, "Peacekeeping Missions: Germany Can Now Play Its Part," NATO Review, No. 5, October 1994, pp. 3–7.

Naumann, Klaus, *Die Bundeswehr in einer Welt im Umbruch* (Berlin: Siedler Verlag, 1994).

Naumann, Klaus, "German Security Policy and Future Tasks of the Bundeswehr," *Defense and International Security*, December 1994, pp. 8–13.

Naumann, Klaus, "Euro-American Security Challenges—Germany's Role and Responsibility," *Transatlantic Brief #9*, July 1994.

Rühe, Volker, *Ressortkonzept zur Anpassung der Streitkräftestrukturen, der Territorialen Wehrverwaltung und der Stationierung* (Bonn: Bundesminister der Verteidigung, March 15, 1995).

Rühe, Volker, *Deutschlands Vertantwortung. Prespektiven für das neue Europa* (Berlin: Ullstein Verlag, 1994).

Rühe, Volker, *Konzeptionelle Leitlinie zur Weiterentwicklung der Bundeswehr* (Bonn: Bundesministerium der Verteidigung, July 12, 1994).

Rühe, Volker, *Weissbuch zur Sicherheit der Bundesrepublik Deutschland und zur Lage und Zukunft der Bundeswehr* (Bonn: Bundesministerium der Verteidigung, 1994).

Rühe, Volker, *Bundeswehr. Sicherheitspolitik und Streitkräfte im Wandel* (Berlin: Verlag E. S. Mittler und Sohn, 1993).

Rühe, Volker, *Verteidigunspolitische Richtlinien* (Bonn: Bundesministerium der Verteidigung, November 1992).